D1639600

000003125175

The
SMALL and MIGHTY
Book of
Space

Published in 2022 by OH!.
An imprint of Welbeck Children's Limited, part of Welbeck Publishing Group.
Based in London and Sydney.

www.welbeckpublishing.com

Design and layout © Welbeck Children's Limited 2022
Text copyright © Welbeck Children's Limited 2022

A CIP catalogue record for this book is available from the British Library.

Writer: Dr Mike Goldsmith, Fellow of the Royal Astronomical Society
Illustrator: Kirsti Davidson
Design and text by Raspberry Books Ltd
Editorial Manager: Joff Brown
Design Manager: Matt Drew
Production: Melanie Robertson

ISBN 978 1 83935 138 9

Printed in Heshan, China

10 9 8 7 6 5 4 3 2 1

FSC
www.fsc.org
MIX
Paper from
responsible sources
FSC® C020056

The
SMALL and MIGHTY
Book of
Space

Dr Mike Goldsmith and Kirsti Davidson

Contents

INTRODUCTION

This little book is full of planets,
moons and more stars than
you can shake a stick at.

All these things lurk high
above the air of planet Earth,
drifting and spinning through space.
Discover how we can explore
them with telescopes,
rockets and robots too.

And find out about . . .

🪐 a space-ghost and space-ghouls

🪐 trees from the Moon

🪐 Santa in space

🪐 why astronauts don't burp

. . . **and lots more.**

Turn the page, and meet the Universe!

Star-Gazing

WHEN YOU LOOK UP AT THE STARS, YOU SEE THEM AS THEY WERE MANY YEARS AGO. THIS IS BECAUSE IT TAKES ALL THOSE YEARS FOR LIGHT TO TRAVEL ACROSS SPACE TO YOUR EYES – AND THERE'S A LOT OF SPACE TO CROSS.

People who study
STARS are called
astronomers, because
"ASTRUM" is Latin
for star.

ASTRONOMERS MEASURE
DISTANCES IN SPACE
BY THE TIME IT TAKES
LIGHT TO CROSS THEM. ONE
LIGHT YEAR IS VERY
ROUGHLY 10 TRILLION KM.

THE SUN

is a **STAR**. It only
looks so much brighter
than other stars because
it's so much closer than
the rest (you should
never look at
it directly).

SUNLIGHT

is made deep inside the Sun, and then takes more than 100,000 years to make its way to the surface. Then sunlight moves very fast indeed, reaching the Earth just 8 minutes later.

In space, light is the **FASTEST** thing there is.

THE SUN

SHINES ON THE EARTH ALL THE TIME, LIGHTING ONE HALF OF IT. IT IS **DAY** ON THAT HALF AND **NIGHT** ON THE OTHER. THE **EARTH** TURNS, CARRYING YOU AROUND WITH IT.

IT TAKES **24 HOURS** TO GO AROUND ONCE. THIS IS ONE NIGHT AND ONE DAY.

IT TAKES **ONE YEAR** FOR THE EARTH TO GO AROUND THE SUN.

THE SKY

is blue during the day because blue light from the Sun spreads all over it. The sky is so bright we can't see the stars during the day, but we can sometimes see the Moon.

When there's not much
LIGHT,
like at night, humans
can't see colours — which is
why the **STARS** look **WHITE.**
In fact they are different
colours from deep **RED**
to **BLUE**-white.

The

STARS

become visible after SUNSET, if
it's not cloudy. You see different stars
at different times of NIGHT, different
times of YEAR, and from different
places on EARTH.

Centuries ago,
ancient people started
to name the patterns
of stars in the sky
(called **constellations**).
Most are people – like

ORION THE HUNTER

– or animals – like

TAURUS THE BULL.

But there is also
a clock, a chisel, and
an air-pump up there.

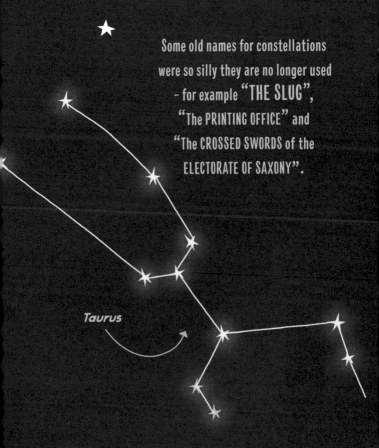

Some old names for constellations were so silly they are no longer used – for example "THE SLUG", "The PRINTING OFFICE" and "The CROSSED SWORDS of the ELECTORATE OF SAXONY".

Taurus

One of the easiest
constellations to find is

ORION THE
HUNTER

- look for the three
stars in his belt.

Orion's belt

SHOOTING STARS
(also called **METEORS**) aren't
really stars – they are bits
of dust falling through the
air from space. They get very
hot and burn up, causing
STREAKS OF LIGHT in the sky.

The brightest starlike thing in the sky
is a planet: our space neighbour

VENUS.

It stays near the Sun, so it can
only be seen at the start
or end of the night.

Venus

Apps and websites tell
you how to find the
planets in the night sky,
as you can't see
all of them every night.
The easiest to see are
VENUS, JUPITER, MARS
and SATURN.

NEBULAS

are cloudy patches in the sky, and there
are many kinds. Some are named after
what they look like - like the
CAT'S EYE, the Horsehead, the
Little Ghost and the WITCH'S HEAD.

The scariest nebula is the

HOURGLASS

- which should really be called
the Giant Scary Eye nebula.

Hourglass
nebula

By **500** BCE people knew that curved pieces of glasses, or lenses, can make things look closer. About 2,000 years later, someone put two of them together to make the first

TELESCOPE.

The year after that, in 1609, **GALILEO** used a telescope to discover new worlds, new stars and new details on the Moon.

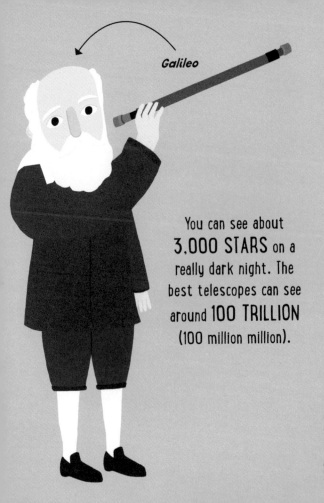

Galileo

You can see about **3,000 STARS** on a really dark night. The best telescopes can see around **100 TRILLION** (100 million million).

The mountain
MAUNA KEA
in Hawaii, USA, is one
of the least cloudy
spots on Earth, so
13 TELESCOPES
have been built there.

Many of the world's best telescopes aren't on Earth at all – they are in orbit around it. There are no clouds there to spoil the view. The best space pictures come from a space telescope called

HUBBLE.

Solar System

Venus

Mercury

Earth

M

Sun

The **SOLAR SYSTEM** is the
Sun, Earth, Moon and other
PLANETS and **MOONS**.
The planet closest to the Sun
is Mercury, and then there
are Venus, Earth, Mars,
Jupiter, Saturn, Uranus
and Neptune.

Jupiter

The planets are named
after ancient gods.
MERCURY, the fastest-moving planet,
is named after the speedy messenger
god. Bright shiny **VENUS** is named
after the goddess of love.
Sea-blue **NEPTUNE** is the name
of an ocean god, and blood-coloured
MARS is god of war.

Uranus

Neptune

Saturn

William Herschel

Although there are eight planets, people only knew about six of them until **1781**, when **ASTRONOMER** William Herschel spotted another one through his homemade telescope. The planet is now called **URANUS**.

William's sister Caroline was an astronomer too. She loved comets, and found lots of new ones.

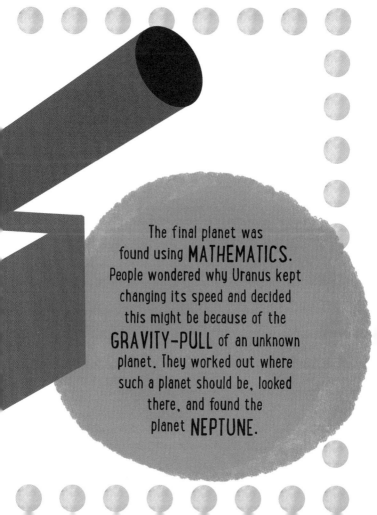

The final planet was found using **MATHEMATICS**. People wondered why Uranus kept changing its speed and decided this might be because of the **GRAVITY-PULL** of an unknown planet. They worked out where such a planet should be, looked there, and found the planet **NEPTUNE**.

The **MOON** isn't a planet: it goes around the **EARTH** rather than the **SUN**. Most of the other planets have moons too.

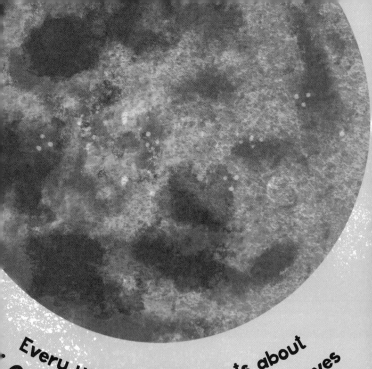

Every year, the Moon gets about CM further from the Earth, and moves round the Earth a little more **SLOWLY**.

Long ago, when the

SOLAR SYSTEM

was new, there were probably
dozens of planets. Some of them
crashed together to form
the eight we know today.

Several moons in the Solar System have **ICY CRUSTS** with huge underground **OCEANS** beneath them. If there are

LIVING THINGS

elsewhere in the Solar System, they may be swimming through these oceans.

AT NIGHT ON

MERCURY,

THE PLANET CLOSEST TO OUR SUN, THE TEMPERATURE IS COLDER THAN A FREEZER. ALMOST AS SOON AS THE SUN RISES, IT SHOOTS UP TO HOTTER THAN AN OVEN, HOT ENOUGHT TO MELT THE METALS LEAD AND TIN.

It can be so cold
and so hot because

MERCURY

does not have a nice thick
atmosphere to spread
the heat around.

For **THOUSANDS** of years, ancient people watched and even **WORSHIPPED** the big bright star seen just after sunset and the big bright star seen just before dawn. But until about 350 BCE no one realised that they are both

VENUS,

the second planet from the Sun.

Venus has such thick **CLOUDS** that its surface is always hidden.

The clouds are made of
SULPHURIC ACID
(a liquid which dissolves metals),
the surface is oven-hot, and
there are probably endless
LIGHTNING storms too.

Every so often, huge ROCKS from space
CRASH onto the Earth. They are called

METEORITES.

As they fall, they make huge BRIGHT STREAKS
in the sky, called fireballs. The biggest
meteorite found so far weighs more
than 60 TONNES (or 10 elephants).

THAT'S QUITE **TEENY**
COMPARED TO ONE THAT **BASHED**
INTO OUR PLANET MILLIONS OF
YEARS AGO. IT THREW UP SO MUCH
DUST THE SUN'S LIGHT WAS CUT
OFF, THE WORLD **FROZE** AND
THE DINOSAURS DIED OUT.

On the

MOON

you could jump six
times higher than on EARTH.

That's because GRAVITY,
which PULLS you down
to the ground, is much
weaker there.

There's **NO AIR** on the Moon.
This means there's **NO WIND OR**
RAIN, the **SKY** is **BLACK** all day
and the stars can be seen **ALL DAY**.

MARS IS SLIGHTLY RED BECAUSE
IT HAS GONE RUSTY. IRON IN THE
SOIL THERE HAS JOINED WITH
OXYGEN TO FORM RUST.

MARS

has weather a bit like
Earth's: sometimes there is
frost or snow, or dust storms.
Dust storms on Mars can
cover the whole planet
for months.

Between Mars and Jupiter
are lots of giant rocks
called ASTEROIDS.
The first asteroid, called
Ceres, was found in 1801,
but at first it was
called a planet.

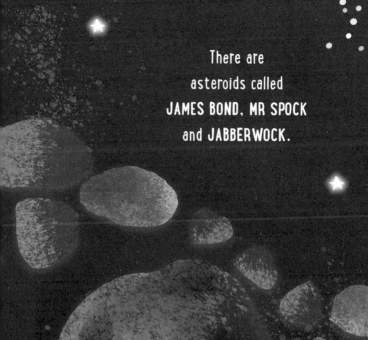

There are
asteroids called
JAMES BOND, MR SPOCK
and **JABBERWOCK.**

It's always stormy on

JUPITER,

the fifth planet from the Sun.
One of these storms is so big
that it can be seen from Earth
with a telescope – people have
been watching the
red swirling storm
for over 300 years.

storm on
Jupiter

JUPITER

is such a big planet
that it weighs more than all
the others added together.

If you spin round fast enough,
your arms will naturally lift up.
A similar effect to this means that
Jupiter, which spins very fast,
bulges sideways and is shaped
like a grapefruit.

SATURN,

THE SIXTH PLANET FROM THE SUN,
HAS ENORMOUS RINGS. THEY
CONTAIN BRIGHT SHINY ICE,
MAKING THEM EASY TO SEE,
THE PLANET IS SO LIGHT
IT WOULD FLOAT IN A BOWL
OF WATER (IF THERE WAS
A BOWL OF WATER
BIG ENOUGH)!

TWO WORLDS
IN THE SOLAR SYSTEM
HAVE LAKES: EARTH,
AND SATURN'S MOON
TITAN. BUT TITAN'S
LAKES ARE BLACK
AND MADE OF
PETROL-LIKE STUFF.

PLANETs ARE LIKE TOPS OR SPINNING COINS. THEY MOVE FROM PLACE TO PLACE (AROUND THE SUN) AND SPIN AROUND AT THE SAME TIME.

URANUS,
the seventh planet,
is different: it
spins on its SIDE.
Probably, another
world CRASHED
into it long ago.

If you were
born on the planet

NEPTUNE,

you would never reach
your first birthday!
Years there are 165
Earth-years long,
because it takes
Neptune that long
to go around
the Sun.

The **STRONGEST WINDS** on Earth blow at about **100 KM** per hour. Winds on Neptune blow 20 times faster than this - **ALL DAY LONG.**

PLUTO

USED TO BE THE NINTH PLANET FROM THE SUN,

BUT IN 2006, **ASTRONOMERS** DECIDED

IT IS TOO TEENY TO BE CALLED A PLANET

AND NOW IT IS CALLED A

DWARF PLANET

INSTEAD.

SOME OF THE MOUNTAINS,
CRATERS AND OTHER
FEATURES ON **PLUTO**
ARE NAMED AFTER PEOPLE
AND THINGS FROM
STAR TREK, DR WHO
AND MONSTERS FROM
HORROR STORIES.

Beyond the planets lie millions of tiny worlds which together form the **KUIPER BELT**. These worlds are called KBOs, short for **KUIPER BELT OBJECTS**.

One **KBO** is nicknamed **SANTA**. It's covered in ice and has two tiny moons called **RUDOLPH** and **BLITZEN**, after the reindeer in the famous poem, "The Night Before Christmas".

Beyond the planets and the Kuiper Belt there is a huge area called the Oort Cloud, full of millions of icy objects like space icebergs.

Sometimes,
objects in the **KUIPER BELT**
or the Oort Cloud start moving
towards the Sun. As they heat up they
STEAM and **BUBBLE**, leaving long tails
of dust and **GAS** behind them. We can
sometimes see them in the
night sky, and we call
them **COMETS**.

In **1994**,
a comet broke into
pieces and fell onto
JUPITER, pulled down
by the strong **GRAVITY**
of the giant planet.

66

Stars

Next time you are on a beach, try
counting the grains in a tiny pinch
of sand. There are MORE STARS in
the SKY than there are GRAINS of
SAND on all the world's beaches.

Most STARS are twins:
PAIRS of stars which go around
each other. But they are so close
that we see each pair as a
single POINT of LIGHT.

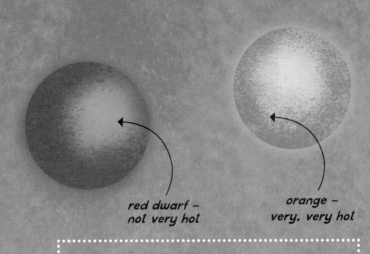

red dwarf –
not very hot

orange –
very, very hot

Most of the stars in the Universe are
small, dim and not very hot. They are called

RED DWARFS.

Even though there are so many red dwarfs, not
a single one can be seen with the naked eye.

Red stars are usually a lot cooler than those of other colours – but still **HOTTER** than an oven. These colours are the ones the stars have when seen through a telescope.

white – spectacularly hot

yellow – ridiculously hot

blue-white – what a scorcher!

Some **STARS** grow and shrink every few days, weeks or months – almost as if they are breathing. They are called variable stars. Two of the oldest ones have names meaning "the **WONDERFUL**" and "the **GHOUL**".

There are **STARS** that have discs around them, which are usually dusty and gassy, but some of these discs are full of **SNOW**.

A lot of
the **MATERIALS** you
are made from come from a
giant **STAR**, which **EXPLODED**
long ago, drifted across space,
and became part of a
SPACE CLOUD.

Eventually,
some bits of the
CLOUD
turned into our
SOLAR SYSTEM –
and, eventually,
YOU.

EXOPLANETS

are planets that go around other stars instead of our Sun. An exoplanet called TrEs-2b is completely black. Another, called GJ 504b, is bright pink, and GJ 1214b is completely covered by an ocean.

55 Cancri E might be made
mainly of diamonds,
while Hd 189733b is
so windy that the rain
falls sideways. And the
rain there is made of glass!

*GJ 1214b in front
of its parent
star*

55 Cancri E

GJ 504b

Our **SUN** is so big that about 1.3 million Earth-sized planets could be squeezed into it. But there are much bigger stars: some are so big that over a **THOUSAND MILLION** Suns could fit inside them. If our Sun was that big, it would cover the whole sky.

The Sun
is about halfway
through its life. In around
5,000 MILLION YEARS
it will get brighter, bigger, hotter
and redder and turn into a
RED GIANT star. Mercury,
Venus and maybe Earth will
fall into the Sun as it swells
into a red giant.

yellow
dwarf

nebula
(star cloud)

red giant

RED GIANTS keep getting bigger until they
have become huge expanding BUBBLES of gas
and dust called PLANETARY NEBULAS.
The "planetary" part of the name
is because they are usually round, like planets.

planetary nebula

white dwarf

AFTER MASSIVE
STARS
DIE, THEY OFTEN LEAVE BEHIND
TINY SHRUNKEN LEFTOVERS CALLED
WHITE DWARFS.
A TEASPOON OF THE WEIRD METAL
WHITE DWARFS ARE MADE OF WOULD
WEIGH MORE THAN A HOUSE.

Once a
WHITE DWARF
has cooled enough to become
dark, it will be a **BLACK DWARF.**
But this **COOLING** takes so long
that not a single black
dwarf exists yet.

Some stars leave behind
objects which are even more
shrunken than white dwarfs, called
NEUTRON STARS or **PULSARS**. Many
of these spin very quickly. They are a bit
like the **SPINNING LIGHTS** on police
cars, but instead of light they
send out beams of
radio signals.

IN 1957, WHEN THE SIGNALS FROM A PULSAR WERE PICKED UP ON EARTH FOR THE FIRST TIME, SOME PEOPLE THOUGHT THEY WERE MESSAGES FROM ALIENS, AND THEY WERE LABELLED LGM FOR

LITTLE GREEN MEN.

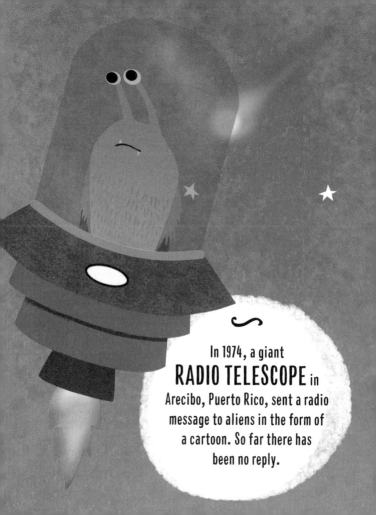

In 1974, a giant **RADIO TELESCOPE** in Arecibo, Puerto Rico, sent a radio message to aliens in the form of a cartoon. So far there has been no reply.

BLACK HOLES

have gravity so strong that
even light can't escape. If
you got close to a black hole,
the gigantic gravity would
pull you out into a long, thin
strand. Scientists call this

SPAGHETTIFICATION.

When the most massive stars die, they explode.

The explosions, called **SUPERNOVAS**, are brighter than whole **GALAXIES**.

Space Travel

People have been
sending objects
that circle, or orbit,
the Earth since the
1950s. These objects are
called **SATELLITES**.
The first, Sputnik 1, was
launched from the Soviet Union
in 1957 (Russia and other countries
were part of the Soviet Union
then). It sent out radio signals
that could be heard all over
the Earth.

One of
the first US
satellites, called
VANGUARD 1,
is still in orbit
today.

DRAGON SPACECRAFT are designed
to take people to space stations.

There are plans to put a hotel in orbit
and take tourists to it in Dragons.

Dragons have special rockets to whisk
them nippily away from danger.

Dragon
Spacecraft

93

WHEN A ROCKET BLASTS OFF, IT GAINS SPEED SO FAST THAT THE **ASTRONAUTS** FEEL UP TO **SIX TIMES HEAVIER** THAN ON EARTH. BUT WHEN THE ENGINES SWITCH OFF, THEY HAVE **NO WEIGHT AT ALL.**

ROCKETS
USE ALMOST **ALL** THEIR
FUEL TO REACH SPACE.
ONCE THERE, THEY **SWITCH OFF**
THEIR ENGINES AND "**COAST**"
FOR THOUSANDS OR
EVEN MILLIONS OF
KILOMETRES.

The first
FILM about an
imaginary Moon
trip was made in 1902.
The ASTRONAUTS
were shot to the Moon
by a CANNON.

Plants have been grown in space, and many ANIMALS have travelled into space, including TORTOISES, JELLYFISH, MONKEYS, SPIDERS, DOGS and CATS.

The word astronaut means **"STAR SAILOR"**, even though astronauts don't go to the stars, or sail anywhere.

Yuri Gagare

The first human space
traveller was Russian-born
YURI GAGARIN,
who travelled around the
Earth in 1961, in a spacecraft
called (in Russian)
SWALLOW.
It was very cramped, and
Yuri was chosen partly
because he was small
enough to fit inside.

In 1961, US President Kennedy decided that Americans would be going to the Moon by 1970. This started a

RACE

with the Soviet Union to get there first.

Saturn V taking off

The race to the Moon was won by the
USA when American ASTRONAUTS
landed on the MOON in 1969.

A lot of **FUEL** is needed for a Moon rocket. Each Apollo rocket (called a **SATURN V**) carried 770,000 litres of fuel, enough to fuel **10,000 CARS.** Most of this fuel was burned up in under **3 MINUTES.**

When the first **ASTRONAUTS** returned from the Moon, they went on a world tour. But first they were put in quarantine for 21 days, just in case they were carrying **MOON-GERMS**.

the crew of Apollo 11

104

In 1971, hundreds of **TREE SEEDS** were taken to the **MOON** and back, and later planted on Earth, to see if they would grow into anything **WEIRD**. Since then, the locations of almost all have been forgotten – they've probably grown to be just the same as normal trees. But you never know . . .

SIX APOLLO SPACECRAFT TOOK 12 PEOPLE TO THE MOON between 1969 and 1972. They left many things behind, including three electric cars and two golf balls.

The **APOLLO**
missions that landed on
the Moon were numbers
11, 12, 14, 15, 16 and 17.
Why no number 13?
Because part of it
BLEW UP
on the way to the Moon,
so the astronauts had to
repair their spaceship
and go home.

MOST SPACESUITS
HAVE 16 LAYERS, AND
TAKE NEARLY AN
HOUR TO PUT ON.
THE INNER LAYER
HAS TUBES
RUNNING THROUGH IT,
WHICH CARRY COOL
WATER SO THAT
THE ASTRONAUT
DOESN'T GET
TOO HOT.

A single **SPACE SUIT** costs over **£10 MILLION**. But without one, an astronaut outside a spacecraft would die a **HORRIBLE** death!

The
WEIGHTLESS
conditions on space
journeys do strange things
to space **TRAVELLERS:**
their bones and **MUSCLES**
SHRINK and weaken, and
they get several centimetres
TALLER. They go back to
normal when they
get home.

In 2018, rocket-builder **ELON MUSK** sent a car into space.

It is still **IN ORBIT** around the **SUN**.

Tortoises, bears, squirrels
and many other animals
SLEEP for weeks or months.
They do this to get through
winter, when food is scarce.
SCIENTISTS are
studying ways for people
to do this too, so they
can make long
SPACE JOURNEYS
to distant planets.

Although **PEOPLE** have only so far reached the Moon, **ROBOT EXPLORERS** have done much better. They have **EXPLORED** every planet in the **SOLAR SYSTEM** and have landed on **MOONS**, **COMETS** and **ASTEROIDS** too.

One of the fastest human-made things is the **VOYAGER 1** space probe, launched in 1977 to **EXPLORE** other planets. It's going 100 times faster than a racing car. Even at that speed, Voyager 1 won't get to a star for over **50,000** years.

Most missions to **MARS** have failed, with the spacecraft **CRASHING** or getting **LOST**. Scientists joke that they are being **EATEN** by a great galactic ghoul.

The first two probes to
land on Mars were called

VIKINGS.

In 1976 they tested the soil on
Mars for life, but the results were so
odd that even now it's not clear
what they found there.

A satellite with people
on board is called a
SPACE STATION.
The first American space station
was called SkyLab. It was launched
in 1972 and was made from a huge
fuel tank originally designed for a
Moon mission that never happened.

In 1979, after six years in space and once all the astronauts had left, **SKYLAB** crashed back to Earth – mostly onto Australia.

There have been people
LIVING in **SPACE**
every day since
2 November 2000,
when the first three crew
members arrived at the
**INTERNATIONAL
SPACE STATION (ISS).**
The ISS was built in
sections, and is still
UNFINISHED.

Burping happens when gas, which is light, **BUBBLES** upwards through the mush inside your stomach, which is heavier. But in orbit (such as in the International Space Station), nothing has weight, so there's no bubbling-up of **GAS**, and **NO ONE BURPS**.

Everything **FLOATS** on a space station,

so toilets are like **VACUUM CLEANERS**,

and suck away astronauts' **POO** and **PEE**.

On the ISS, astronauts sleep on the walls –

their sleeping bags are **STUCK IN PLACE**

so they don't drift around.

The
Universe
and its
Galaxies

OUR SUN is one
of a group of millions of
stars called a galaxy.
Our galaxy is called the
MILKY WAY,
and is one of many millions
of galaxies, stretching
out through space.

~

The word **GALAXY**
comes from the Greek
word for milk, because
the Milky Way looks like
someone has spilt milk
across the night sky.

The **UNIVERSE** is the name given to all the **GALAXIES,** and everything else, too. Most of the stuff in the Universe is invisible. It is called **DARK MATTER.** No one knows what it is made of.

The **MILKY WAY** is a spiral galaxy. There are lots of other spiral galaxies, and many other shapes too.

The
SOMBRERO GALAXY
looks like a hat, with
a brim made of dust.
(A sombrero is a hat
with a wide brim.)

People who STUDY
the UNIVERSE
aren't called universologists –
they're called
COSMOLOGISTS,
because "cosmos" is
another word for Universe.

Most space objects are very old.
The **EARTH, SUN** and **MOON**
are more than
4,000 MILLION
years old, and the
whole Universe is about
three times older than that.

One day,
the **MILKY WAY**
will collide with another galaxy,
called **ANDROMEDA**. But,
because stars are so far apart,
very few will actually
CRASH into each other.

There is
a lot of **DUST**
in space. On a very
dark night you might see
that the Milky Way has dark
STRIPES running along it.
These are made of **CLOUDS**
of dust, getting in
the way of stars
behind them.

Most galaxies,
including ours, have
BLACK HOLES
in the middle, often millions
of times more massive
than the Sun.

They are called
SUPERMASSIVE
BLACK HOLES.

The **MICE** are
a pair of galaxies that
COLLIDED long ago. They
are now moving apart again,
but a long **MOUSE-TAIL**
of **STARS** still
connects them.

A GALAXY
called the Tadpole
also has a long
STAR-TAIL.

137

The **UNIVERSE**
began nearly 14 billion
(that's 14 thousand million)
years ago, in a sudden burst
of energy called the

BIG BANG.

The brightest things in the Universe are **QUASARS**. They are huge flares of **LIGHT** from things falling into black holes in distant galaxies.

〜

One **QUASAR** is surrounded by a **CLOUD**. Like clouds on Earth, it is mostly made of **WATER** – about 100 billion times as much as in our oceans.

The
UNIVERSE
is bigger today
than it was yesterday,
and will be even
BIGGER
tomorrow.

Ever since the
BIG BANG,
the Universe has
been **GROWING.**

No one knows
if or when this

**EXPANSION OF
THE UNIVERSE,**

as it is called,
will stop.

COSMOLOGISTS
have different ideas about
how the **UNIVERSE** will
end in the very far
distant **FUTURE.**

Some think that it will freeze,
others that it will tear itself
to pieces, and a few
that it will all crunch
up together.

And
maybe then
it will start all
over again . . .